Beyond the Roll Book

Sunday School and Evangelism

Diana L. Hynson
Scott J. Jones

A Workshop for Congregational Leaders

Copyright © 2006 by Abingdon Press. All rights reserved.

With the exception of those items so noted, no part of this work may be reproduced or transmitted in any form or by any means, electronic or mechanical, including photocopying and recording, or by any information storage or retrieval system, except as may be expressly permitted by the 1976 Copyright Act or in writing from the publisher.
Requests for permission should be addressed to Abingdon Press,
201 Eighth Avenue, South, P.O. Box 801,
Nashville, TN 37202-0801.

Scripture quotations are taken from the *New Revised Standard Version of the Bible,* copyright © 1989, Division of Christian Education of the National Council of the Churches of Christ in the United States of America. Used by permission. All rights reserved.

06 07 08 09 10 11 12 13 14 15—10 9 8 7 6 5 4 3 2 1

Scott Jameson Jones serves as Resident Bishop of the Kansas Area of The United Methodist Church. Prior to his election in 2004, he served as pastor of four congregations and as Associate Professor of Evangelism at Perkins School of Theology. His most recent books are *United Methodist Doctrine: The Extreme Center* and *The Evangelistic Love of God* and *Neighbor: A Theology of Discipleship and Witness*, (both Abingdon Press).

Diana L. Hynson is Director of Learning and Teaching Ministries at the General Board of Discipleship in Nashville, Tennessee. Dr. Hynson is an elder in the Baltimore-Washington Annual Conference and holds an M.Div. and D.Min. in Christian Education from Wesley Theological Seminary in Washington, D.C. Rev. Hynson held several appointments in local churches before moving to Nashville. She worked for many years as an editor at The United Methodist Publishing House before moving to her current appointment. Diana serves on the board of the national Christian Educators Fellowship.

Special thanks to the Foundation on Evangelism for the grant that made this project possible.

At the time of publication, all websites were correct and operational.

Contents

Planning Your Workshop 4

Segment 1: Know Your Bible 9
Keep the Main Thing the Main Thing

Segment 2: Know Your Context 14
Everybody Has to Be Somewhere

Segment 3: Know Your Potential 16
Be All You Can Be

Segment 4: Know Your Destination 18
If You Don't Know Where You're Going, Any Road Will Do

Appendix

Worksheet 1: Congregational Inventory 20

Worksheet 2: Community Change 21

Worksheet 3: Church and Community Data 22

Worksheet 4: Congregational Trajectory 23

Worksheet 5: Appreciative Inquiry 24

Worksheet 6: SWOT Analysis 25

Worksheet 7: What If … ? 26

Worksheet 8: Guiding Questions 27

Worksheet 9: Our Action Plan 28

Alternative Schedules 29

Sunday School: It's for Life! Resources 30

Sunday School and Evangelism Resources 31

Planning Your Workshop

Evangelism

Evangelism implies

- **reaching out;**
- **engaging in service** that witnesses to Jesus Christ;
- **inviting others** to the fellowship of the church;
- **welcoming new persons** into the family of faith.

Within the church, evangelism is a ministry when members tell their stories to one another and nurture one another's growth.

Outside the church, evangelism is critical in helping persons who are searching, unchurched, or dechurched find a welcome and a home within the household of faith.

By **"unchurched,"** we mean those who have had no significant exposure to or experience with an organized local church or religion.

By **"dechurched,"** we refer to those who have had exposure or experience that was negative enough to drive them away or not compelling enough to encourage them to remain.

A lump of clay, a chunk of granite, or a pile of girders will always be a lump, chunk, or pile until it is formed into a beautiful lamp, an exquisite sculpture, or a magnificent skyscraper. With deliberate attention and skill, these raw materials become something wondrous. The prophet Isaiah used the image of God as potter and of us as clay to note that we require God's hand in our spiritual formation (Isaiah 64:8). New Testament writers suggested that churchgoers will only just "suckle milk" without the "meaty" experiences that form us into mature Christians who reach our God-given potential in faith and godly service (1 Corinthians 3; Hebrews 5). The skyscraper doesn't build itself; and in true Christian community, we don't build ourselves. We pay attention and offer intentional guidance to one another. We learn and grow in community.

Purpose and Goals

The Sunday school—and all the small groups in the church—are places rich in the potential for faith formation, disciple making, and evangelistic outreach. Every single class, group, or event in your church is at its heart an opportunity to invite others to share in the life of Christ—and that is evangelism. This workshop will help you and your leadership group look *beyond* the roll book to strengthening your Sunday school, especially for evangelism.

This workshop offers you several goals or outcomes:

- gaining a biblical and theological foundation for building a strong Sunday school and evangelistic outreach;
- reviewing the current cultural context of your church and community;
- examining your current reality and the potential of your Sunday school; and
- creating an action plan for greater ministry through your Sunday school.

Beyond the Roll Book: Sunday School and Evangelism

The Workshop Organization

The workshop will have four parts:

1. Keep the Main Thing the Main Thing—Know Your Bible
2. Everybody Has to Be Somewhere—Know Your Context
3. Be All You Can Be—Know Your Potential
4. If You Don't Know Where You're Going, Any Road Will Do—Know Your Destination

This workshop is intended for about two hours. The basic plan will generally use only the **core activities,** which are mostly discussion oriented. You may find that one of the **expansion activities** seems better suited for your group than a core activity, or you may decide to add one to the basic plan. Feel free to choose among all the options to create an experience that works best for your needs.

A two-hour workshop will have limits. You may benefit from having more time. **Expansion activities** allow the group to go much deeper. Consider using these activities in addition to the core ones to create a multisession workshop.

Segments 2 and 3 include a brief **video presentation** from the enclosed DVD by Bishop Scott Jones of the Kansas Area. Bishop Jones was speaking at a Sunday school and evangelism event in Kansas. The presentations are ten and seven minutes respectively. A synopsis of each is set apart in the margin of the corresponding segment's opening page.

On pages 19–29, you will find **reproducible handouts** for working on the core activities, expansion activities, and subsequent action planning. These worksheets are also on the DVD so that you can print them for your group.

The final three pages offer lists of helpful resources. Web materials include the link, which you can access through the DVD. Printed materials may be ordered through Cokesbury, and the link to the electronic bookstore is on the DVD.

This workshop will provide a foundation for strengthening your Sunday school, but most of your efforts will be devoted to following through on the insights, discoveries, and needs that have been identified by the end of the workshop. The workshop will get you started on an **action plan**, with planning and process tools to aid you. Segments 1, 2, and 3 lead you to the action planning in Segment 4. Monitor your time and pace so that you get to the action steps as the end.

Alternative Plans

Each of the segments is outlined and organized so that it can be used as an independent session in an expanded, multisession workshop or retreat. The expanded plans offer more time for preliminary assessment and subsequent planning. Suggested alternative schedules are on page 29.

Planning Your Workshop

Preparation Checklist

In advance:
- ☐ Plan ahead.
- ☐ Be clear about the purpose and goals.
- ☐ Decide on the participants.
- ☐ Publicize and recruit.
- ☐ Recognize the mutual support for worship and education.
- ☐ Establish prayer partners for all participants.
- ☐ Invite a co-leader.
- ☐ With your co-leader, read through the entire Leader Guide, and preview the DVD.

The week before:
- ☐ Have the participants do pre-meeting work.

The day of the workshop:
- ☐ Have all of your supplies on hand.
- ☐ Make the space comfortable and inviting.
- ☐ Provide food.

In Advance

Plan ahead. Establish a timeline for what you want to happen, when you want it to happen, how long it will take to do, who will do it, and who will evaluate how well it achieved its purposes. Reserve your space and the date on the church calendar to make sure that the day and place are available and do not compete with anything else that requires the same participants. If you plan on holding this event away from the church, locate and reserve that space well in advance. Take into account the rules regarding food and use of the space. If you need to coordinate carpooling, plan on doing so.

Be clear about the purpose and goals. Then communicate them. Include them in your publicity and the invitation to participants. Write out the goals and purpose of the workshop on a large sheet of paper, and post it in the room. (See the list on page 4 as your starting point.)

Decide on the participants. An essential first step is to determine who are key decision makers in your congregation and who are persons with gifts for analysis, planning, follow through, and motivating others. They may hold official roles or responsibilities related to the Sunday school or evangelism, or they may simply be just the "right" ones for this task at this time. Such persons include:

- pastors
- paid and volunteer education staff, including daycare or weekday ministry leaders
- church council chairperson (with the support of the whole council)
- education ministry chairperson
- evangelism ministry chairperson
- Sunday school teachers
- small group leaders
- age-level leaders
- Sunday school superintendent
- youth group officers
- other interested class or group participants (including youth and young adults)

The importance of the pastor's presence and support cannot be overestimated. The Sunday school and evangelism directly affect how well persons are nurtured spiritually as faithful and effective disciples. If the pastor is not a workshop leader, he or she should be encouraged to be on the team and to attend the entire workshop. Being in attendance and taking seriously the function and potential of the Sunday school is an important, validating gesture.

Publicize and recruit. Make this opportunity known in as many ways as you can imagine, including announcements during worship. Invite people to indicate their interest. Consider these ideas for letting people know about the workshop:

- church bulletin announcements
- postings on bulletin boards
- announcement in classes and small-group gatherings
- e-mail
- church newsletter
- recognition of planners in worship
- prayer vigil for the ministry of the Sunday school

Personally talk with those folks you have identified. No series of announcements or general publicity will have the same results as a personal invitation!

Recognize the mutual support of worship and education. Encourage the pastor and other worship planners to highlight this workshop opportunity during worship services. Corporate worship is the one place where the whole church gathers consistently to hear the Scriptures read and proclaimed. The Sunday school and other faith-forming groups offer the best opportunity for dialogue, questions, and deeper focus on the meaning and application of the biblical text. Our outreach and invitation to the community (and church members) can only be strengthened when the members are well grounded in the Bible and other Christian spiritual formation activities that are learned and practiced through the Sunday school and small groups.

Establish prayer partners for all participants. Undergirding all ministries with prayer is a vital practice. Consider partnering persons in the congregation who are not a part of the educational ministry with those who will attend the workshop. Such a partnership is a fruitful way to receive the gift of service from older adults who have difficulty getting out. You might also ask the children and youth to pray for their teacher or group leaders.

Invite a co-leader. Although the workshop is only two hours, having at least two persons in leadership allows those leaders to be participants for part of the time. Two or more leaders also offer variety in style and multiply the enthusiasm among the rest of the group.

With your co-leader, read through the entire Leader Guide, and preview the DVD. Select the plan you want for each segment, swapping expansion activities for core activities as you think appropriate. Decide which activities each of you will lead.

Planning Your Workshop

Supplies

- nametags
- large sheets of paper
- markers of at least three colors
- participant list
- Bibles
- *The United Methodist Hymnal*
- index cards
- DVD player
- red, yellow, and green sticky dots, or multiple markers in those colors
- copies of the handouts for each person

Sacred Space

Setting up a focal point as a worship center will remind the participants that they are there to work on ministry and to achieve God's desires for all of us to be formed as faithful disciples.

The Week Before the Workshop

Have the participants do their pre-meeting work. Ask them to read Matthew Chapters 21–28 in advance. You may also choose to send them copies of pages 12 and 13 so that they can read and reflect, having the additional information at hand. This step will "prime the pump" and help discussion flow more readily when the group meets. Encourage them to bring their Bibles and something for note taking.

In addition, ask them to jot down these two simple assignments and bring them to the workshop:

- one gift or strength that they bring to the education ministry of the church, one gift or strength that they see in one of the other participants, or both. You might provide a participant list to each person in advance, so that he or she knows who is attending.

- a brief summary of their best Sunday school or small-group experience from any age. The summary should note what happened and why it was significant.

Invite the participants to support this event and ministry in prayer and to pledge to follow through on the results of the workshop.

The Day of the Workshop

Have all of your supplies on hand. The specific supplies needed for each segment are listed in a box on the segment's opening page.

Make the space comfortable and inviting. Workshop participants will need a room large enough to sit at tables without crowding. If possible, use a room that has enough wall space to put up newsprint and enough floor space to move around. Ensure adequate light, heating, cooling, and ventilation, as well as comfortable chairs.

If at all possible, arrange the room so that the participants sit in small table groups of four to six people, so that they can hear one another for small-group activities and have room to take notes.

Using some table décor to create a focal point adds visual support to the content and experience of the workshop. You might invite the participants to place a personal item or religious symbol there; or ask the church or leadership team to provide those items.

Provide food. Considering the time of day, you may want to have light refreshments or a meal before or after your time together. Most of us ask for healthy snacks and then eat the doughnuts and chocolate. Nevertheless, plan for a variety of foods that take into account both taste preferences and health concerns.

Segment 1

"Keep the Main Thing the Main Thing"
Know Your Bible

> **Time:** 15 minutes for Welcome; 20 minutes for Bible Study
>
> **Goal:** To get acquainted and gain a biblical and theological foundation for building a strong Sunday school and outreach
>
> **Supplies:** nametags, markers, Bibles; optional: hymnals, index cards
>
> **Preparation:** Copy the Bible Study (pages 12–13) for the group members. Post the purpose and goals.

Welcome: Core Activities

1. **Make nametags.** As the participants arrive, ask them to make a nametag with their name, the grade or group they lead, and how long they have been a leader (or participant) in that group.

2. **Mingle.** Serve refreshments (if you wish), and encourage the group members to circulate a bit to get acquainted before the workshop begins. Invite them to tell brief stories of their Sunday school experiences.

3. **Review the purpose and goals.** Point out the posted statement, and clearly communicate what will happen. Review the flow of the workshop through each segment.

4. **Share gifts, strengths, and prayer.** Ask the participants each to offer a five- to seven-word description of the gift or strength they bring or that they see in another participant. Then pray for the workshop and one another.

Welcome: Expansion Activity

A. **Play an icebreaker game.** Ask each person to say briefly either one thing he or she appreciates about or desires for the current Sunday school or small group or one wonderful memory, from any age or place, about a Sunday school or small-group experience. Each response must be different.

Nametag
Have your nametag on as a model.

> Name
>
> Grade or Group
>
> Length of Time in Role

Segment 1: Know Your Bible

Know Your Bible: Core Activities

5. **Distribute copies of the Bible study (pages 12–13).** In just one or two minutes, set the context of the three Matthew passages by summarizing the Overview on the handout. Your time and discussion will be enhanced if your group members have read and reflected upon the passages beforehand. (See page 8.)

6. **Study the Bible.** Form three groups, and assign one of the focal passages to each group. Ask each group to read or skim the Matthew text, background information, and sidebar comments that apply.

7. **Discuss the Bible passage.** Within each group, discuss and respond to these questions, which you may wish to write on a large sheet of paper or reproduce on a small sheet for each group:

    - What is the "main thing" in the passage?

    - What do we know about God and Jesus from this passage?

    - What is the lesson of discipleship we can take from the passage?

    - What does the passage ask of you (and how prepared are you to embrace that calling)?

    - What does the passage state or imply about the link and importance between Sunday school and evangelism (including outreach and service)?

    - How is God with you?

8. **Compare the findings.** Gather together to talk about these questions:

    - What do these things suggest to you about the importance of your present Sunday school and small-group offerings?

    - What are the main things you get from this study?

    List them on a large sheet of paper for further reference during the workshop.

Our Wesleyan Heritage

John Wesley considered evangelism a "work of mercy" just like feeding the poor, visiting the sick, and so forth.

Know Your Bible: Expansion Activities

B. Define the terms. In your context, how would you describe "nations," "neighbor," "the least," and "disciples"? How would you describe yourself as member of the nation, as neighbor, as the least, and as a disciple? How does your relationship to the church change (if it does) with each role? How well equipped is your church to go to "all nations," to minister to "the least," and to "disciple" one another and those outside?

C. Sing a love song. Distribute copies of *The United Methodist Hymnal,* and search for a hymn that exemplifies how you would like to love God and neighbor. (See the suggestions to the right.) What is the theology of the hymn text? How does the hymn move or inspire you to love? Sing a few of the selections. What stands in the way (if anything) of being able to love radically as Matthew 22 requires?

Hymn Suggestions
- "Christ for the World We Sing," No. 568
- "Go, Make of All Disciples," No. 571
- "O Zion, Haste," No. 573
- "The Church of Christ, in Every Age," No. 589
- "Rescue the Perishing," No. 591
- "Here I Am, Lord," No. 593

D. Separate the sheep from the goats. Note that service—reaching out to others—was the sole criterion for achieving eternity in God's kingdom. Establish one side of the room as "Inherited the Kingdom" and the other side as "Cast Into Eternal Fire." Ask the participants to move to the place along that imaginary line between the two sides that best illustrates the state of their present practice or that of their Sunday school class or small group.

Ask:

- What does that placement tell you?
- How does outreach fit in your class or group plans?
- What changes might bring you closer to the Kingdom, and what would it take to implement them?
- What sense of responsibility does your class or group have for reaching beyond its walls and boundaries?

E. Explore doubts and fears. Distribute index cards to each person. Ask the participants to write down one major doubt or fear that inhibits their ability to teach and evangelize in "all nations." Gather and shuffle the cards; then select them in turn. Talk about how together you can dispel fears and doubts or use them positively. How can you keep your eye on the main thing, free from distraction? How is God with you, and how are you with God?

Segment 1: Know Your Bible

1   Bible Study: The Main Thing

The Big Picture

This study focuses on passages from Matthew 22, 25, and 28. To set the context, read beginning with Matthew 21, Jesus' entry into Jerusalem and end with Matthew's post-Resurrection report to the Eleven (Chapter 28).

Love

For Christians the meaning of the word *love* in reference to God and to neighbor comes from the understanding of God's nature made known in Christ. From this perspective we come to know love as unconditional and unlimited. Such love is not a matter of feeling but of commitment and action.

"The Neighbor" and "The Least of These"

Matthew 22 identifies "neighbor" according to Leviticus 19:18, which suggests someone within the Hebrew community. Likewise, the Hebrew Scriptures are clear about the treatment of the "least" among their tribes and among the sojourner in their midst.

In these Matthew passages, however, Jesus is pushing his hearers to expand their minds and hearts. Where once "neighbor" and "least" were closer to home, now they extend to "all the nations," which ultimately will be joined as one in God.

Overview

From the time of Jesus' entry into Jerusalem, he was beset by controversy, which he fueled by his actions, teachings, and comments, beginning with his cleansing of the Temple (Matthew 21:12-17) and his enigmatic curse of the fig tree (21:18-22). People questioned his authority, and the scribes and Pharisees had their first unsuccessful go at him. His subsequent question about the two sons, his parable of the wicked tenants, and his parable of the wedding banquet (21:23—22:14) raised considerable anger among the chief priests and Pharisees, who recognized that Jesus' strong (and even condemnatory) remarks were directed at them.

Matthew then begins a concentrated section of verbal sparring (22:15-33, 41-45) in which the Pharisees and the Sadducees pose questions as traps. First is the question about paying taxes to Caesar (a question answered with a question), then a query about the Resurrection (answered with the diversion that they didn't know what they were talking about), and then a question from Jesus about David's son (a trap for the Pharisees and Sadducees).

The Great Commandment (Matthew 22:34-40)

The Pharisees go at Jesus again. They ask in falsely flattering terms, "Which commandment in the law is the greatest?" It appears as if Jesus offers two commandments instead of the one for which he was asked. First, love God with heart, soul, and mind; and secondly, love neighbor as yourself. Yet his comment, "a second is like it" asserts equality, not similarity; both parts of the same commandment have equal weight. Loving God and neighbor are not two distinct acts but one inseparable one.

The parallel passage in Mark 12:28-34 shows the lawyer implying the same understanding. Taking both commands as one unit, he asserts that it is "much more important that all whole burnt offerings and sacrifices" (12:33). Luke's report of this comment is a prelude to the parable of the Good Samaritan, in which we examine the meaning of the word *neighbor*. In this story, the lawyer asks, "What must I do to inherit eternal life?" Jesus led him to the Great Commandment (Luke 10:25-28).

Taken together, we see that loving God and neighbor is one thing, which is more important that the entire prescribed practices of worship and which is the source of eternal life.

© 2006 by Abingdon press. Permission is granted for the purchaser to reproduce this page for use with BEYOND THE ROLL BOOK.

Bible Study: The Main Thing

The Great Judgment (Matthew 25:31-46)

The passage between the Great Commandment and the Great Judgment includes warnings, woes, laments, and parables that describe what will come in the Last Days. The climax is the parable of the separation of the "sheep" (the righteous) from the "goats" (the unrighteous) and the description of the clash of kingdoms: the true Kingdom (of God) and the false kingdom.

The nations will be judged at the last day, and the sole criterion for entry into God's kingdom or banishment to an eternal damnation is the care of "the least of these." There is no mention of belief, faith, grace, justification, or forgiveness of sin. At this judgment, both the "sheep" and the "goats" are surprised at this criterion. The sheep did not recognize that service to "the least" is the same as service to Christ; the goats did not recognize that service was important for any reason. Furthermore, in light of Jesus' other comments to the Jewish authorities, the "goats" would be surprised to find out that they weren't "sheep."

We learned from the various reports about the Great Commandment that the stakes are high; the Great Judgment affirms that failure to love God and neighbor leads to death, regardless of one's position or authority.

The Great Commission (Matthew 28:16-20)

Following the Great Judgment, Matthew reports all of the events from the plot to kill Jesus to the Resurrection. The one who had modeled love of God and neighbor lost his earthly life in the clash of kingdoms, yet he reunited as the risen Lord one more time (according to Matthew) with his remaining eleven disciples.

Matthew reports that "some doubted" (Matthew 28:17), but doubt is not unbelief; rather, it indicates an imperfect faith. Yet Jesus expected his followers to assume some of his authority and go to "all nations" to "disciple" them, baptize, and teach (which they had not done before). "All nations" are neighbors, and the whole community is to love one another.

Discipling includes doing the works that Jesus had done. Jesus promises to be with us through the power of the Holy Spirit to bring those works to fruition. (See also John 14:11-13.) The "innocent" righteous may have done (godly) works unaware, but now the call and commission is clear, overt, and obligatory.

"The Nations"

The term *nations* is often translated as "Gentiles." But in this context, as God brings everything into one, having ultimate control, the nations include *both* Jew and Gentile. In addition, the meaning refers not to the institution of the church or government but to each individual who makes up the nations.

Doubt and the Disciples

Even those who experienced the Resurrection firsthand struggled with doubt. Their faith was not perfect. Yet, it is not to angels or perfect believers but to the worshiping/wavering community of disciples that Jesus gives his commission to reach the world.

For Reflection:

- What is the "main thing" in each passage?
- How might it relate to Sunday school and evangelism?

© 2006 by Abingdon press. Permission is granted for the purchaser to reproduce this page for use with BEYOND THE ROLL BOOK.

Segment 2

"Everybody Has to Be Somewhere"
Know Your Context

Key Points from the DVD Presentation

- **Loss of Christendom:** For a time in the United States, Christianity was culturally dominant. Social customs supported worship attendance and participation in Sunday school. That support no longer exists in most areas of the country.

- **Biblical Ignorance:** The earliest of the Boomer Generation was generally "churched" and had some understanding of the Bible. These characteristics can no longer be taken for granted for subsequent generations.

- **Digital Culture:** With cell phones, e-mail, the Internet, iPods, and DVDs, communication isn't what it used to be. Keeping up requires some investment. The divide widens between those churches that use the latest modes of communication and those that don't.

- **Loss of Community:** Church and family have both turned inward and have fragmented so that they are not the cohesive relationships they once were.

Time: 30 minutes

Goal: To review the current cultural context of your church and community

Supplies: DVD, DVD player, large sheets of paper, markers, and a pencil for each person

Preparation: Preview the DVD. For each person make a copy of Worksheet 1; Optional: Worksheets 2, 3, and 4 (pages 20–23).

Know Your Context: Core Activities

9. **Play the DVD.** Form small groups, and ask them to listen especially to what the presentation says about the loss of Christendom, biblical ignorance, digital culture, and loss of community. At the end of the presentation, discuss these questions:

   - How true are these cultural shifts for our church, families, and community?
   - What do our "main thing" Bible passages say about our context?
   - How can reflecting on the cultural shifts from past to present help us map out our future?

10. **Examine the "mosts."** Write each of the four points (left margin) as a heading on a separate sheet of large paper. Ask the groups to identify for each the most startling, distressing, encouraging, and urgent implication or information. Record the responses on the sheets. For each list, come to consensus on the one or two responses that seem the most important. Keep the list.

11. **Complete an inventory.** Use Worksheet 1: Congregational Inventory (page 20). This inventory is a forced choice list of questions that asks you to rank your level of agreement with each question. Tabulate the inventory by adding the ranked numbers for each question and dividing the total by the number of responses. (For example, six people might answer Question 1 with a 5, 4, 5, 6, 2, and 3 respectively, for a total of 25 and an average of 4.2.)

    - What do your average results tell you about your context and readiness for strengthening Sunday school and evangelism?

Know Your Context: Expansion Activities

F. Map out changes in your community. Distribute copies of Worksheet 2: Community Change (page 21).

Ask the participants to use this worksheet to create a timeline mapping out the change in your community. The starting point is your first day in your current community. Using increments of one year, three years, five years, or whatever increment you choose, note the changes to the community and when they occurred. Think about population growth or decline, relationships among neighbors, communication patterns, growth or decline of school and businesses, patterns of integration, social changes, growth and decline of churches, church membership, and so on.

When you are finished, compare maps and your collective memories. Discuss these questions:

- What portrait emerges, and what implications does it have for you for the future?
- Given your current portrait, how could, would, or should you reach out to persons and incorporate them into the body of Christ through your Sunday school?

G. Do census research. Assign this task to someone or a small team to do in advance of your meeting. Ask the person or team to get official data from the US Census (*www.census.gov*), in addition to searching their collective memory, for information about the community. The US Census can provide population data, economic data, and much more. A record of changes in your church or annual conference are available at the Statistical Reports over the course of several years. The Conference Journals may be in your church office and will be on file in the conference office. In addition, the General Council of Finance and Administration of The United Methodist Church maintains records for the entire denomination (*www.gcfa.org/RecordsandStatistics Page.htm*).

Have the person or team use Worksheet 3: Church and Community Data (page 22) and bring the information to the meeting for discussion.

H. Chart where you are headed. If you continue to do what you've always done, you will continue to get the same results. Worksheet 4: Congregational Trajectory (page 23) gives the group an opportunity to imagine other possibilities. Pass out a copy of this sheet to each participant, and have the participants work on it either individually or in pairs or threes as they prefer. The chart will begin to capture ideas about where you are, where you want to be, and what to consider in order to achieve the future that you believe God desires for you.

Websites

- US Government Census (*www.census.gov*)

- Look for your conference office website by searching (*www.umc.org*). From the Regional Offices dropdown box, select Annual Conferences.

- GCFA statistics (*gcfa.org/RecordsandStatistics Page.htm*)

Segment 2: Know Your Context

Segment 3

"Be All You Can Be"
Know Your Potential

Synopsis of the DVD Presentation

Intent: The original intent of Sunday school was evangelistic. Seeing the "street urchins," caring Christians responded by creating "school" to change the lives of poor children. Sunday was for many children, the only day they weren't working.

Place: Churches have the facilities, and people are already on site for worship.

Functions: Sunday school is a

- source of faith knowledge
- builder of Christian community
- loving environment
- shaper of faithful habits
- context for evangelism

Tell Stories

"My senior high Sunday school class was great because the leader took every question seriously and helped me think through my beliefs."

(twenty-two words)

*You can read the entire article and see an alternative series of questions at www.gbod.org/ education/articles.asp? item_id=10557.

Time: 25 minutes

Goal: To examine the current reality and the potential of your Sunday school

Supplies: DVD, DVD player, large sheets of paper, and markers of at least three colors. Optional: stick-on dots of three colors

Preparation: Preview the DVD. For each person, make a copy of Worksheet 6 and either Worksheet 7 or 8 (pages 24–27).

Know Your Potential: Core Activities

12. **Play the DVD.** Together listen especially for

    - the original intent,
    - the privileged place, and
    - the functions of Sunday school.

    Ask:

    - How do these ideas compare with to the intent and functions of your Sunday school?
    - What aspects of your Sunday school need strengthening?
    - What functions are you doing that were not mentioned?
    - How do the "main thing" Scripture passages help you think about the key functions of your Sunday school?

13. **Tell stories.** Ask volunteers to describe, in about twenty words, their best Sunday school or small-group experience from any age in their lives and why is was so good. (The point is to get at the success factors quickly, not to share lengthy histories.) How many of the stories relate to the key points from the DVD? List the success factors on a large sheet of paper, and keep it for reference.

14. **Ask questions.** Ask yourselves, "What if…?" questions. Read through Worksheet 7, "What If…? (page 26). You do not need to discuss all of the questions. Start with the ones that seem most relevant to your situation or that capture your imagination.

    Or use the Guiding Questions on Worksheet 8: Guiding Questions (page 27), which is an adaptation of "(The First) 45 Guiding Questions to Assess the Education Ministry of Your Church."*

Know Your Potential: Expansion Activities

I. Take a SWOT at your classes and groups. Use Worksheet 6: SWOT Analysis (page 25). Strengths and weaknesses are things that are under the direct influence of the church or class (such as teacher recruitment and training). Opportunities and threats are things that may affect the church or class but over which you have only indirect influence, if any (such as population migration in or out of the community).

Work in small groups to do the analysis for each age level.

Then, on a large sheet of paper, compile a master SWOT chart, doing the analysis for your Sunday school and small groups as a whole. Together identify as many factors for each category as you can. (If something seems to fit in more than one place, list it again.)

Now give each person a set of three markers or stick-on dots that are each red, yellow, and green. Tell the participants the SWOT-dot code. (See the right-hand margin.) Then have them put a dot next to the items on the master list.

When everyone has marked the data, calculate the score for each item on the list. Add five points for each green dot, and three for each yellow dot. For each red dot, subtract 1. The sums will tell you where most of the energy (positive and negative) is for the issues important to the Sunday school. Note how many of what color are posted for any given item. If something gets several green and red dots, it may come out near the top of the list but have stiff opposition as well.

Highlight the most important items that help you understand the potential of your classes, groups, or church.

J. Engage in a brief appreciative inquiry. (This activity is a good alternative to Activity 13 ("Tell stories").) Use Worksheet 5: Appreciative Inquiry (page 24). The same things that drew you to and keep you involved in your Sunday school may appeal to others. Ask the participants to jot down, at the beginning of the timeline, what it was about their Sunday school or small-group experience that compelled them to join.

Ask:

- What did you like, appreciate, and value that brought you there? Be as specific as you can about the reasons. (You might add these qualities to your success factors.)
- What has kept you involved? Why?
- What positive values and practices do you want to take into your future, or what sort of legacy are you leaving for the next generation?

SWOT-Dot Code

- The **green dot** means, "This is important, and I want to spend time and energy on this."
- The **yellow dot** means, "This has relevance but doesn't excite me. I won't work against it."
- The **red dot** means, "This isn't important at all to me. I won't engage in it and may oppose it."

Appreciative Inquiry

The entire process is much lengthier. For more information, see, for example, *Appreciative Inquiry Handbook: The First in a Series of AI Workbooks for Leaders of Change* (paperback), by editors David L. Cooperrider, Diana L. Whitney, and Jacqueline M. Stavros (ISBN 1576752690). This resource is available through Cokesbury.

Segment 4

"If You Don't Know Where You're Going, Any Road Will Do"
Know Your Destination

> **Time:** 30 minutes
>
> **Goal:** To identify the next steps for follow through on an action plan for developing or strengthening your Sunday school
>
> **Supplies:** A calendar
>
> **Preparation:** Gather all the data sheets from the previous segments. Make a copy of the Sample Action Plans (next page) and Worksheet 9 (page 28) for each person.

Know Your Destination: Core Activities

15. **Pick five.** Review the findings from the day. Examine the various sheets of paper you've posted of your work thus far. All together identify five main issues or ideas that you feel strongly about.

16. **Choose your priorities.** Look at the group's list again. Ask, Which of these is too long-term? Cross it off the list—at least for now. Ask, Which of these is the most expensive? Cross it off the list—at least for now. (In your follow up, come back to those items.)

17. **Develop your action plans.** Divide into three groups, one for each of the remaining three priorities. In the groups, talk about your desired outcome or goal, what things can be done to achieve that goal, what things must be avoided in order to succeed, what the next steps are, and who will be responsible for those. On the next page is a form with two examples. These examples will be helpful, but feel free to write your action plan in a way that makes sense to you. Use worksheet 9 (page 28).

18. **Commit to the plans.** Report your action plans to the whole group; ask for additional suggestions and volunteers. Set a time for completion or reporting. As you close the session, return to the Scriptures you studied, summarizing the connections to your decisions. Close with prayer for God's continuing guidance.

19. **Evaluate.** Evaluate the workshop. Start with these questions:
    - What went well?
    - What did we hope to achieve that is not yet completed?
    - What new learning did you gain?

Evaluation Questions

In addition to the three general questions to the right, you can also evaluate your satisfaction with the following:

- preparation for the event;
- the facility and space;
- leadership;
- readiness of the group to tackle the purpose;
- adherence to the stated purpose;
- ability of leaders and participants to grasp and deal with the relevant issues to achieve the goals;
- the usefulness of the study guide, DVD, and process.

Beyond the Roll Book: Sunday School and Evangelism

Sample Action Plans

A Focus: letting people know what's available in Sunday school

Steps:

1. **Decide the best way(s) to get the information out to church members, visitors, and the community.**

    In order to **decide**, *(assigned to_____ by when _____)*,

    - we need to find out costs and what financial resources are available
      (assigned to_____ by when _____).

    - we need to identify possible resource persons in the congregation
      (assigned to_____ by when _____).

2. **Create something specific, such as a brochure, e-mail plan, Web presence, or news article.**

    In order to **write or design**, *(assigned to_____ by when _____)*,

    - we need to gather information and testimonials about the various classes and offerings
      (assigned to_____ by when _____).

    - we need to take photos and we need to have photo releases signed
      (assigned to_____ by when _____).

B Focus: doing a better job of caring for people enrolled in Sunday school

Steps	Who	When	Barriers to break down to be successful	Who needs to have ownership	Measures of success
Know who is enrolled (bring roll books up to date, or establish a system for recording attendance).					
Communicate to teachers the importance of keeping attendance records as a way of knowing who's missing and then extending care to them.					
Establish system for following up on persons who are absent twice in a row.					
Provide tools and training (postcards, e-mail addresses, phone numbers) to designated persons for follow-up caring.					
Measure attendance for increases.					
Evaluate follow-up system; decide refinements.					

© 2006 by Abingdon Press. Permission is granted for the purchaser to reproduce this page for use with BEYOND THE ROLL BOOK.

Worksheet 1

Congregational Inventory

Rank each statement from 1–6 according to your level of agreement. 1= no, not at all; 6 = yes, always. Do not deliberate on an item; just choose your first impression.

1. Our church is growing; leadership and structure are keeping up with growth. 1 2 3 4 5 6

2. Our community is growing. 1 2 3 4 5 6

3. We have a plan within the church that takes into account the growth, stability, or decline of our community.

4. My church is a great place, and I want to invite others. 1 2 3 4 5 6

5. Our leaders intentionally nurture their spiritual growth and expand their biblical knowledge. 1 2 3 4 5 6

6. We have Sunday school or other small-group opportunities for all ages. 1 2 3 4 5 6

7. I am satisfied with the church's Sunday school ministry for children, youth, and adults. 1 2 3 4 5 6

8. We communicate so that persons can find out about classes and groups easily. 1 2 3 4 5 6

9. Class and group members know how to be open and hospitable to one another and to newcomers. 1 2 3 4 5 6

10. Visitors are welcomed and helped to find their way around. 1 2 3 4 5 6

11. We do a good job of inviting and recruiting teachers and leaders. 1 2 3 4 5 6

12. We do a good job of supporting and training our teachers and leaders. 1 2 3 4 5 6

13. My class or group helps me learn the Bible and practice spiritual disciplines. 1 2 3 4 5 6

14. I receive support and accountability for my Christian growth in my class. 1 2 3 4 5 6

15. My comfort level with evangelism (talking about my faith with someone else) is (1=low; 6= high). 1 2 3 4 5 6

16. We do a good job of getting names and contact information from visitors and members. 1 2 3 4 5 6

17. We have a system for following up with visitors and with absent members. 1 2 3 4 5 6

18. Our nursery is clean, inviting, safe, and staffed by the same trusted people each week. 1 2 3 4 5 6

19. Our building is accessible for older adults and for persons with disabilities. 1 2 3 4 5 6

20. Church members are good about leaving parking spaces close to the entrance ways for visitors. 1 2 3 4 5 6

© 2006 by Abingdon Press. Permission is granted for the purchaser to reproduce this page for use with BEYOND THE ROLL BOOK.

Worksheet 2

Community Change

Create a timeline of significant events in the life of your church and community. Start with the year you either entered the community or the church, whichever was earlier. On each line above the timeline, indicate events, changes, or circumstances you felt had a positive influence. On the lines below the timeline, indicate events, changes, or circumstances that you felt had a negative influence. Think about population growth or decline, relationships among neighbors, communication patterns, growth or decline of school and/or businesses, immigration, integration, social changes, growth and decline of churches and church membership, and so on. Add as many lines as you need.

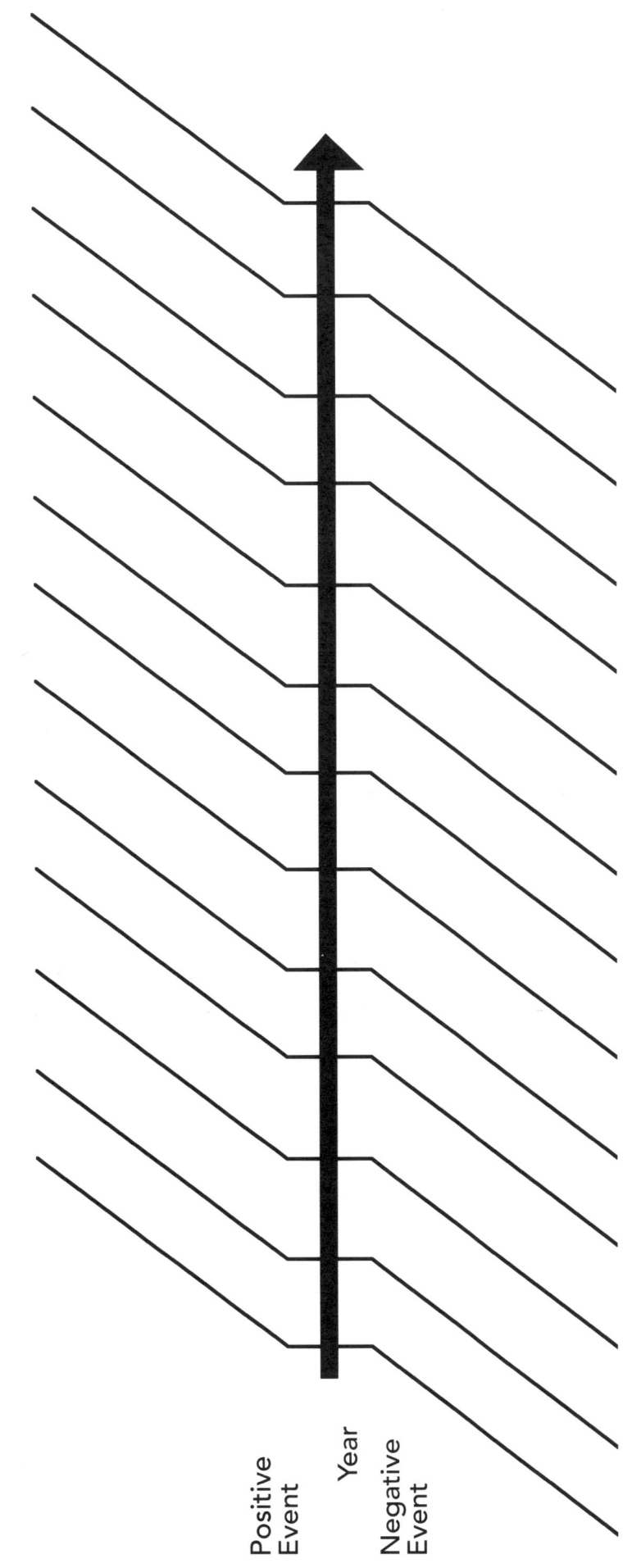

Positive Event

Year

Negative Event

© 2006 by Abingdon press. Permission is granted for the purchaser to reproduce this page for use with BEYOND THE ROLL BOOK.

Worksheet 3

Church and Community Data

Use the Conference Journals, your annual statistical reports, data from the General Council of Finance and Administration, information from the US Census, and your own knowledge of your local church history to compile as much of this information as you can. Information from Worksheet 2 may be helpful here. Record information from your peak years and in five-year increments before and after (unless you are now at your peak) for each applicable item. Look for trends and factors that could have an impact on your church.

1. Your church membership and number of baptisms and professions of faith (How do those numbers compare to other churches in the district?):

2. The number of participants in Sunday school classes, small groups, and mid-week groups (How do those numbers compare to other churches in the district?):

3. Population of your county or community, as well as number of persons at different ages (such as a "graying" of the population):

4. The racial profile of the residents in your community compared to your membership profile:

5. Economic factors in the community, such as average income, spending, and saving ability:

6. Shifts in economy and local business base:

7. Location and level of home or highway construction that have (or could have) an impact on the church or community:

8. Changes in the schools that have (or could have) an impact on the church or community:

Other:

© 2006 by Abingdon Press. Permission is granted for the purchaser to reproduce this page for use with BEYOND THE ROLL BOOK.

Worksheet 4
Congregational Trajectory

Consider your current practices and policies that relate to your Sunday school and evangelism. Think about the specific classes and groups; who leads them; how up-to-date the leaders are in current educational and leadership practice; how you nurture their growth (or not); whether classes and groups are available for the whole life span (at least what is represented among current members) and for persons who are at early, mid, and late maturation in their faith. Factor in other issues that are relevant for you. This whole collection of information becomes the portrait of your system. Your system will achieve the results it is designed to achieve; so if your ministry is going well, you have a good system. If not, look more closely at your system.

Step 1: What results are we currently getting?

1. _____
2. _____
3. _____
4. _____

Step 2: What results do we desire?

1. _____
2. _____
3. _____
4. _____

> If we continue to do the same things, we'll continue to get the same results.

Step 3: What changes from what we are currently doing (and what new steps) do we need to implement to reach our desired results?

_____
_____
_____
_____
_____
_____
_____

© 2006 by Abingdon Press. Permission is granted for the purchaser to reproduce this page for use with BEYOND THE ROLL BOOK.

Worksheet 5

Appreciative Inquiry

Use this simplified Appreciative Inquiry tool to concentrate on the positive things that you have appreciated about your experience with your **Sunday school class or small group**.

Date I Started _____   **Midpoint Date** _____   **Now** _____

What attracted me. I liked, valued, appreciated these things	What has kept me involved and why	The positive values to take to the future; what legacy
1.	1.	1.
2.	2.	2.
3.	3.	3.
4.	4.	4.
5.	5.	5.
6.	6.	6.
7.	7.	7.
8.	8.	8.
9.	9.	9.
10.	10.	10.

© 2006 by Abingdon Press. Permission is granted for the purchaser to reproduce this page for use with BEYOND THE ROLL BOOK.

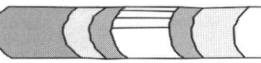 # Worksheet 6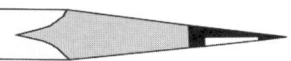

SWOT Analysis

List the **strengths, weaknesses, opportunities,** and **threats** of your Sunday school classes and small groups.

STRENGTHS: internal; within your control	**OPPORTUNITIES:** external; outside your control
WEAKNESSES: internal; within your control	**THREATS:** external; outside your control

© 2006 by Abingdon Press. Permission is granted for the purchaser to reproduce this page for use with BEYOND THE ROLL BOOK.

Worksheet 7

What If...?

Use these questions to spark your imagination:

1. What if every children's, youth, or adult Sunday school class were so meaningful that the participants wanted to come and were eager to tell other people about their Sunday school experience?

2. What if children, youth, and adults were regularly encouraged and expected to invite others to Sunday school? (Eighty percent of people visit a church because someone invited them.)

3. What if when visitors came, the class members were intentional about greeting and including them in ways that made them feel welcomed and at home? What if Sunday school classes evaluated their hospitality and figured out ways to improve the experiences of visitors?

4. What if when visitors came, church members were available to greet them and escort them to the appropriate Sunday school classes or the nursery?

5. What if six or so members of one class agreed to be "glue people" who started a new class and invited persons who came to worship services only or persons from the community to come and be part of the new Sunday school class?

6. What if the church were intentional about making vacation Bible school, a special children's event, or an after-school ministry an outreach program and aggressively publicized it in the neighborhood?

7. What if Sunday school teachers and others followed up with repeated invitations to the VBS or after-school ministry participants and their parents? What if congregational members were assigned to be "the church family" or the "pew buddy" for any children who came without parents?

8. What if Sunday school classes identified and followed through with a service project that would have some visibility in the area and be a witness to the church as well as to Christ's love?

9. What if we offered "Sunday school" or other small groups at times other than Sunday morning? What if we offered a Parent's Day Out program and a Bible study for parents during the same time? How else might we use our facilities during the week?

10. What if we offered a "beginnings" class for newcomers to the faith? What if we offered classes that probe into the deeper questions of faith?

11. What if we found ways to help members "tell their faith stories" so that they became more confident in inviting others to be a part of the community of faith?

12. What if within forty-eight hours someone from the church made contact with first-time visitors? A five-minute conversation at the doorstep, especially with a gift of something homemade, can make a great impression.

If you want one of these scenarios to be true for your church and it isn't, what would it take to make it so?

© 2006 by Abingdon Press. Permission is granted for the purchaser to reproduce this page for use with BEYOND THE ROLL BOOK.

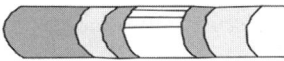 # Worksheet 8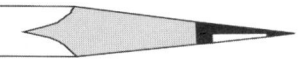

Guiding Questions

1. Do you have a vision statement for the Christian education and formation ministry of the church? Does it get checked and updated as needed?

2. Do you have an overall learning plan rather than a collection of learning options? Is there an understanding that the goal of the learning plan is faith formation and disciple making that is evidenced in daily life?

3. Do you have groups or classes based on the biblical or theological development of the participants? (For example, do you have "entry level" Bible study classes for youth or adults, as well as "intermediate" and "upper level"? Do you have "entry level" groups for people completely new to the Christian faith, as well as groups that probe into the deeper faith questions for more mature believers?)

4. Do you consider leadership training and development to be a part of the educational ministry of the church?

5. Are there any barriers to participation, such as accessibility issues (mobility, sight, hearing, comprehension level), transportation, and timing?

6. Do you have teachers and leaders for each needed education and formation group or class? Do you not offer needed groups because of lack of leadership?

7. Do you have any set criteria by which you evaluate the teacher or leader's qualifications (such as demonstration of Christian character, good rapport with the age group, proven teaching skills, and responsibility and dependability in attendance and preparation)?

8. Is the pastor involved in (or supportive of) the Sunday school? Does he or she make available the fruits of his or her biblical and theological education to the teachers and leaders? Does the pastor take interest and active involvement in "upper level" Christian education and formation opportunities that require or would benefit from the pastor's theological and biblical expertise?

9. Do you have ways to evaluate whether the programs, classes, ministries, and faith-formation opportunities make any impact? (These measures include things such as reported change in lifestyle, cultivation of Christian practices, attendance and participation patterns, growth toward leadership positions, acceptance of healthy mentoring opportunities, and greater depth of personal relationship with God.)

10. Do you have in place a sufficient and working policy for the safety and protection of leaders and participants? Do you do security checks on people who work with people under age eighteen? If not, why not? Do you have adequate insurance and liability coverage? How recently has your insurance been reviewed?

11. Are rooms clean, well lit, and equipped with supplies necessary to the lesson?

12. Is the space attractive enough to be inviting to guests?

These questions are adaptations and excerpts from "(The First) 45 Guiding Questions to Assess the Education Ministry of the Church," by Diana L. Hynson. © 2004 by the General Board of Discipleship of The United Methodist Church. Used by permission. To see the entire article, visit *www.gbod.org/education/articles.asp*.

© 2006 by Abingdon Press. Permission is granted for the purchaser to reproduce this page for use with BEYOND THE ROLL BOOK.

Worksheet 9

Our Action Plan

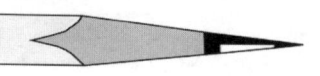

Create your action plan. Write it in any form that makes sense to you and serves your needs. State your focus, desired outcome, or goal. Then consider these questions:

- What steps will it take to get there?
- What one thing must happen in order to achieve our goal?
- Who needs to be "on board" or have ownership?
- Are there any barriers to overcome?
- Is there anything to avoid in order to succeed?
- What will be the measure(s) of success?
- Who will take responsibility for this step?
- By when should it be completed?
- To whom do we report?

© 2006 by Abingdon Press. Permission is granted for the purchaser to reproduce this page for use with BEYOND THE ROLL BOOK.

Alternative Schedules

Overnight Retreat Schedule

- **Evening (7:00–8:30)** Use the "First Meeting" (list in the right-hand column).

- **Morning (8:30–12:00)** Use both the "Second Meeting" and the "Third Meeting," but add a break between them.

If the retreat is longer, build in more time for fellowship, worship, conversation, and relaxation. You may also be able to have small groups begin the steps to carry out their action plans.

3 or 4 Weekly Meetings

- **For 3 consecutive meetings,** follow the outline at the right, perhaps saving Expansion Activity A of the welcoming activities for the beginning of the second meeting and adding Expansion Activity C for the beginning of the third meeting.

- **For 4 consecutive meetings,** follow pages 9–19 and incorporate more of the Expansion Activities.

Since sessions in these options are separated by time, be sure to build in welcoming and a more extensive review each session to get folks back on board with one another, the work done to date, and the process.

First Meeting (1½ hours)

1. Make nametags.
2. Mingle.
A. Play an icebreaker game.
3. Review the purpose and goals.
4. Share gifts, strengths, and prayer.
5. Distribute Bible study pages.
6. Study the Bible.
7. Discuss the Bible passage.
8. Compare the findings.
B. Define the terms.
9. Play the DVD.
10. Examine the "mosts."

Second Meeting (1½ hours)

Welcome and Brief Review

11. Complete an inventory.
F. Map out changes in your community.
G Do census research *(from an advance search)*.
H. Chart where you are headed *(optional)*.
12. Play the DVD.
13. Tell stories *(and/or J. Appreciative Inquiry)*.
14. Ask questions.
I. Take a SWOT at your classes and groups.

Third Meeting (1½ hours)

Welcome and Brief Review

15. Pick five.
16. Choose your priorities.
17. Develop your action plans.
18. Commit to the plans.
19. Evaluate.

© 2006 by Abingdon Press. Permission is granted for the purchaser to reproduce this page for use with BEYOND THE ROLL BOOK.

Sunday School—It's for Life! Resources

Use the inviting "Sunday School—It's for Life!" logo to help promote your church's Sunday school program. To create professional-looking custom messages, FREE templates on select products are available to download from *Cokesbury.com* when you enter the item number. Call Curric-U-Phone at 1-800-251-8591 for details.

Certificates of Appreciation. Recognize the outstanding work of a teacher, coordinator, Sunday school superintendent, or volunteer worker. Imprint these flat 11" x 8½" certificates on your computer with the FREE downloadable template.
Item # 0687491703. Package of 12.

Postcards. An easy way to drop a note to a teacher, class member, or potential member to tell the person he or she was missed or inform the person of a coming event.
Item # 0687491606. Package of 25.

Posters. Large, colorful posters are a great way to spread the message that Sunday school is important. Great for hallways, classrooms, or fellowships halls. Posters are 10½" x 16½".
Item # 0687334527. Set of 12.

Business Cards. Promote your Sunday school with these customizable cards—a simple, attractive, and non-threatening way to invite people to Sunday school. The colorful logo is printed on one side; customize the back with a message from the church, a particular Sunday school class, or an individual. Includes 10 sheets with 10 cards on each; 100 total. A FREE computer template is available.
Item # 0687491401. Package of 100.

Door Hangers. The logo on this door hanger sends a clear message that Sunday school is an exciting place where newcomers feel at home. The reverse side is blank; download a FREE template to customize this space with your church's custom invitation. Includes 10 sheets with 4 door hangers on each; 40 total.
Item # 0687491509. Package of 40.

 sundayschool.cokesbury.com

Beyond the Roll Book: Sunday School and Evangelism

Sunday School and Evangelism Resources

The Celtic Way of Evangelism: How Christianity Can Reach the West...Again, by George Hunter III. Abingdon Press, 2000; ISBN 0687085853.

Evangelism in the Small-Membership Church, by Royal Speidel. Abingdon Press, 2007; ISBN 0687335795.

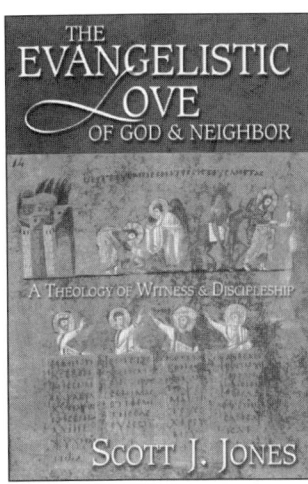

The Evangelistic Love of God & Neighbor: A Theology of Witness & Discipleship, by Scott J. Jones. Abingdon Press, 2003; ISBN 0687046149.

Foundations: Shaping the Ministry of Christian Education in Your Congregation. Discipleship Resources, 1993; ISBN 0881771236.

How to Reach Secular People, by George Hunter III. Abingdon Press, 1992; ISBN 0687179300.

I Knew Them All by Heart, by Myrtle Felkner. Discipleship Resources, 2006; ISBN 0881774774.

Keeping in Touch: Christian Formation and Teaching, by Carol F. Krau. Discipleship Resources, 1999; ISBN 0881772488. Also available in Spanish: *¡En Contacto!: La Formación Cristiana y la Enseñanza.* ISBN 0881774294.

Leader in Christian Education Ministries (quarterly magazine from Cokesbury). To subscribe, e-mail *subservices@abingdon.com* or call 1-800-672-1789.

Loving God With All Your Mind: Equipping the Community of Faith for Theological Thinking, by Thomas R. Hawkins. Discipleship Resources, 2006; ISBN 0881773980.

The Ministry of Christian Education and Formation: A Practical Guide for Your Congregation, by Donna Gaither, Mary Alice Gran, Susan Hay, Betsey Heavner, Diana Hynson, and Carol Krau. Discipleship Resources, 2003; ISBN 0881773956.

Needs-Based Evangelism: Becoming a Good Samaritan Church, by Robert D. Pierson. Abingdon Press, 2006; ISBN 0687332486.

The Race to Reach Out: Connecting Newcomers to Christ in a New Century, by Michael J. Coyner and Douglas Anderson. Abingdon Press, 2004; ISBN 0687066689.

Radical Outreach: The Recovery of Apostolic Ministry and Evangelism, by George Hunter III. Abingdon Press, 2003; ISBN 068707441X.

Sacred Bridges: Making Lasting Connections Between Older Youth and the Church, by Mike Ratliff. Abingdon Press, 2002; ISBN 0687063663.

Sacred Challenge: Blazing a New Path for the Sunday School of the Future, by Mike Ratliff. Discipleship Resources, 2006; ISBN 0881774790

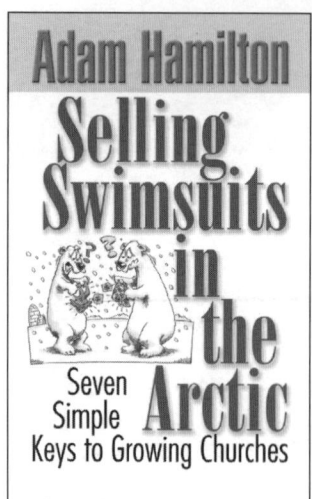

Selling Swimsuits in the Arctic: Seven Simple Keys to Growing Churches (paperback), by Adam Hamilton. Abingdon Press, 2005; ISBN 0687343844.

Selling Swimsuits in the Arctic: Seven Simple Keys to Growing Churches (leadership kit), by Adam Hamilton. Includes a hardcover copy of the original text. a leader's guide, a DVD, and CD-ROM; participants can use the paperback version of the book. Abingdon Press, 2006; ISBN 0687333938.

Seven Ways of Teaching the Bible to Adults: Using Our Multiple Intelligences to Build Faith, by Barbara Bruce. Abingdon Press, 2000; ISBN 0687090849.

Triangular Teaching: A New Way of Teaching the Bible to Adults, by Barbara Bruce. Abingdon Press, 2007.

United Methodist Doctrine: The Extreme Center, by Scott J. Jones. Abingdon Press, 2002; ISBN 068703485X.

What Every Teacher Needs to Know About series: *The Bible, Christian Heritage, Classroom Environment, Curriculum, Faith Language, Living the Faith, People, Teaching, Theology,* and *The United Methodist Church.* Discipleship Resources, 2002. Available as a set of each title (ISBN 0881773743) or a set of ten copies of a single title.

Witness: Exploring and Sharing Your Christian Faith, by Ronald K. Crandall. Discipleship Resources, 2003; workbook and journal set ISBN 0881773220; video ISBN 0881773549.

Websites and Curriculum Resources

The General Board of Discipleship

Christian education: www.gbod.org/education

Evangelism: www.gbod.org/evangelism

Spiritual formation: www.upperroom.org

Congregational leaders: www.gbod.org/congregational

The United Methodist Publishing House

www.sundayschool.cokesbury.com. Look here for ways the pastor and others can support the Sunday school. Click the link for "promote the Sunday school."

www.cokesbury.com. One key help for strengthening the Sunday school is good curriculum resources. Click on Cokesbury Finder. This interactive service will help you find the resources that fit your needs.

iLeadYouth.com. This website gives free samples of various resources, plus access to real persons you can talk with about curriculum needs and other issues related to youth ministry, including the Sunday school.

Contact also **curricuphone@umpublishing.org** or **800-251-8591** to talk with knowledgeable and friendly Christian education consultants. Their service is also free and extremely valuable. Talk with them about curriculum or any other subject related to the Sunday school and evangelism.